The Ra
Velo city

Carter Hayn

Rosen
REAL
READERS

Rosen
Classroom™
New York

Let's go to the **racetrack**! There is more
than one type of racetrack. Some tracks
go in a straight line. Some go in a circle.

Cars that race in a straight line go in only one **direction**. These cars start a race at a speed of zero. They finish the race very fast.

Race cars gain **speed** quickly. They can go from zero to over three hundred miles per hour in only a quarter of a mile.

The speed of a race car and its direction give you its **velocity**. Velocity is speed plus direction.

This race car is going in only one direction. It can only change its velocity by changing its speed. If it speeds up or slows down, it has changed its velocity.

Some racetracks are in the shape of an oval. On this kind of track a race car must change direction. The car can slow down or speed up. The car can also turn in another direction.

There are different ways to change velocity. When this car crashed, it lost a lot of speed. It also changed direction. It lost velocity.

A tow truck comes to carry away the car.
The velocity of the car will change again.

Great drivers can control their speed
and direction. They will win the race.
The drivers who can't control speed and
direction will fall behind.

Speed gets us places fast. Direction makes sure we get to where we want to go. Velocity wins the race!

Glossary

direction   The course along which someone or something is moving.

racetrack   A course for racing.

speed   How fast something is moving.

velocity   The speed of something plus the direction it is heading.